Just think about it!

What's this book all about then?

How can I find the loot on page 18 when all these words are missing?

How do I know who caught which fish on page 20? There are too many to choose from.

These pictures of Howling Hank on page 7 don't make sense.

Aren't they hopeless? You do have to <u>think</u> while you're reading!

★ Why don't you look at the activity on page 7 about Howling Hank? If you read the story, you'll see how to put the pictures in the right order.

★ And what about those missing words on page 18? You need to read the letter and look at the map — then you can work out the missing words. Finding the loot is then really easy.

★ You'll soon be able to work out the fishy puzzle on page 20. First you read the descriptions of the fish each of the B-Team caught. Then you'll be able to match the words to the right fish. Now all you've got to do is draw the fishing lines!
All the things in this book will help you practise **thinking** about what you read.
Thinking about what you read is what comprehension is all about.
When you do comprehension at school you sometimes have to read passages and answer questions. Answering questions is one way of helping you to think. You'll find ways that are more fun in this book.

If you do the activities in this book, you'll find comprehension at school mega easy. Just think about it!

Crossed wires

Our class is having a sale tomorrow. Claudia, Lisa, Sid and Paul are helping me to organise it. We each have to ring someone to make sure they bring the things they promised. Help! All the wires are crossed!

*Can you draw in the telephone wires to show who is talking to whom?
We've done the first one for you.*

CLAUDIA
Have you made the mince pies yet? We need them tomorrow.

MARK
Yes, I'll bring them but there's still a lot of dirt on them.

RESHMA
Can you bring in those flower pots you promised?

KENG-TAK
Sorry, I can't get them. My dad's still wearing them.

LISA
Have you got those old carpet tiles you said we could have?

WEEDY WEASEL
Oh dear, I forgot. I'll make them now and put them in the oven before school tomorrow.

SID
Have you got the goldfish you were going to let us have?

TATTY TRICIA
I'm sorry, my mum's changed her mind. She wants to put them down on the bathroom floor.

PAUL
Did you remember to get those old trousers for the old clothes stall?

ALI
I've got them, but I haven't got enough jam jars to put them in.

Could you sort out who was talking to whom? If you did, you were **matching** the questions and answers. See if you were right by looking at page 22.

3

Mixed-up rooms

Skulk, take this letter and get rooms ready for these important guests.

6, Shivering Street,
Ghoultown,
GH9 4 SS
2nd January

Gargoyle's Guest House,
3 Rodent Avenue,
Ghoul End,
Gloomshire ZK3 48K

Dear Mr. Gargoyle,

I would like to book some rooms at your charming guest house for myself and four friends. We will arrive tonight. Please give me a very damp and cold room. I must have slimy, running water also a leaking shower and mouldy walls if possible. Mr. and Mrs. Haunt would like a large room with cobwebs, moving pictures, creaking floors and a skeleton in the cupboard. Mr. Dungeon would like straw and chains in his room. Please also provide a few rats and some dry bread and water. Mr. W.E.R.E. Wolf would like a room with a kennel, some bones and an electric fan to keep off the flies.

Yours sincerely
Augusta Leech

Skulk gives the guests the keys to their rooms.

MR. & MRS. HAUNT   33

MRS. LEECH   34

MR. DUNGEON   31

MR. W.E.R.E. WOLF   32

The guests don't seem very happy with the rooms they've been given!

ROOM 31

Groan! This is damper than the Tower of London!

ROOM 32

I wanted some bones to chew, not live rats! Help!

ROOM 33

There isn't room for two in here!

I don't like this wind!

ROOM 34

Oh dear! No running water. I wish that picture would keep still!

Skulk has got the rooms mixed up! **Can you sort them out? Put the correct room number on each key.** *You'll find the answers on page 22.*

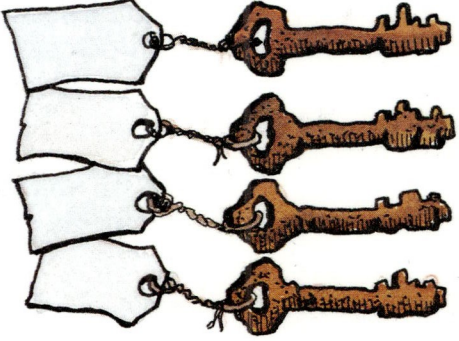

MRS. LEECH

MR. & MRS. HAUNT

MR. W.E.R.E. WOLF

MR. DUNGEON

This is about **matching** writing and pictures.

Read the letter.

Compare what it says with what the pictures tell you, and then, for ghouls' sake, put the guests in the right rooms.

5

Howling Hank

Howling Hank sets off across the mountains on his old mule.

'Oh my darling, oh my darling, oh my daaaaarling Clementine . . .' he sings.

The sun is blazing down. Hungry vultures fly overhead. They are waiting for Hank to die! But Howling Hank sees nothing of this. He is thinking about the gold.

'Giddy-up Max! A few more days and I'll be the richest hound in the West!'

A few days later he arrives.

'Here at last. And down to our last drop of water too. This must be the place. Now to start digging. Come on, Max. This looks like a good spot.'

Meanwhile, unnoticed by Hank, an evil-looking figure creeps up. It is his enemy, Powerful Pete!

'You're on my land, hound,' he roars. He kicks Hank high into the air. Max stops chewing for a moment. He watches as Howling Hank zooms through the air and lands on a giant cactus.

'Oweeeeeeeeeeee . . . !'

These pictures from a cartoon film about Howling Hank have got muddled. *Can you put them in the right order? Write the right number for each picture in the box.* We've done the first one for you.

OH MY DARLING

You'll find the right order on page 22. Learning about history is like this. You've got to get things in the **right order** or else . . .

The dogs of Olan

Why don't you read this story? You can find the missing words on the other page. Be careful!

Loda pulled her cloak around her. The wind was icy. She kept running. She was out of breath.

At last she caught up with Fane. 'Wait,' she ...., 'Wait. I can't go any further.'

Fane gave her his hand. He was also very weak. She could only just hear his voice. 'We have to go on,' he .... 'We can't stop now.'

They walked on up the steep mountain path. Rocks blocked their way. Suddenly Fane slipped. Loda watched in horror as he fell into the mist. 'Fane,' she .... , 'Fane, where are you?'

She climbed down the rocks. Fane lay at the bottom. He was holding his leg. His face was white with pain.

'It's broken,' he .... , 'I can't move it. You'll have to go on without me. You must reach the City before dark.'

Loda shook her head. She started to cry. 'No, no,' she .... , 'I can't leave you here to die!'

Fane took her hand. 'Loda, please, please,' he .... 'You must go. We must save the City. You must warn them that Olan is coming.'

Loda stood up. 'I will go, but I will come back. I will bring help,' she ....

8

Olan was peering into his tele-viewer. He started to grin and then his huge body shook. 'Poor fools,' he .... 'So you think you can save the City! No-one can escape Olan! I am Olan the Great, Olan the Terrible, Olan the Mighty!' he ....

He rang the great, brass bell. Two men ran into the room. Olan's voice made them tremble. 'Send out the Dogs,' he .... , 'Send out the Dogs! Let the Dogs of Olan find them!'

Can you fill in the gaps? *You could put 'said' in each gap but that would be boring. Here are ten better words. Choose the word **you** think is best for each gap. Look carefully for the **clues.***

begged	promised	boasted
roared	groaned	screamed
laughed	sobbed	panted
	whispered	

Roxy Rockstar's diamonds

Hatchet and I won a voyage on a ship in a raffle last week! Who was in the cabin next to ours but Roxy Rockstar! You know how rich she is, don't you? We spent ages planning how to steal that diamond necklace she always wears.

Which plan will work?

Plan A
I know, boss. Wait till she goes to bed, then press the fire alarm. She'll rush out to the lifeboats. We'll go into her cabin and grab the necklace. No problem.

Plan B
No, we'll use my diamond-finding suction tube. She'll put the necklace on the table at night. We'll feed the tube out of our porthole and into her's. It will suck up the diamonds from the table. No noise! No fingerprints!

Plan C
No, no. This is what we should do, boss. There's a fancy dress disco in the cafeteria tomorrow night. Roxy's going dressed as a banana. I'll go as a gorilla. You turn the lights off and I'll unzip the banana and grab the necklace.

Plan D
No, I know. We'll dress up as Lord and Lady Somebody. We'll sit at her table at dinner. She's sure to invite us back to her cabin for a drink. When we're there we'll tie her up and steal the sparklers.

Of course all the plans went wrong — just look what happened!

1. Can you put the letter for each plan by the side of the picture which shows what went wrong with the plan? Look at page 22 to check your answers.

2. Now can you write down the **reason** why each plan went wrong? We've left you space to do this here.

Plan A went wrong because	
Plan B went wrong because	
Plan C went wrong because	
Plan D went wrong because	

Have you **matched** our plans and the pictures? Have you written down what went wrong? Then you've spotted the **cause** of each disaster.

11

Sid's food machine

My brilliant machine turns two potatoes and a packet of vege sausage and burger mix into an instant meal!

This is how the machine works:

1.	Put two potatoes in the spud-washer. They will be washed here.
2.	You can choose how you want your potatoes by pressing a button on the potato selector. You can have chips, mash or baked.
3.	Empty the packet of vege sausage and burger mix into the splodger. It will be mixed with water.
4.	You press a button on the other selector to choose sausages or burgers. You press the red button if you want Shepherd's Vege Pie.
5.	The potatoes are peeled and cut into chips in the slitter.
6.	The baked potatoes go straight to be baked in the scorcher.
7.	In the squisher the potatoes are cooked and mashed.
8.	The chips are fried in the frazzler.
9.	In the burger-basher, the vege mix is shaped into burgers.
10.	In the banger-basher, the vege mix is rolled into sausages.
11.	For Shepherd's Vege Pie the vege mix is put into a pie dish in the pie-plonker.
12.	The mashed potato travels down the gulley into the pie-plonker. Here it goes on top of the vege mix.
13.	The burgers and sausages are grilled in the sizzler
14.	The Shepherd's Vege Pie is baked in the scorcher

SPUD-WASHER   POTATO SELECTOR

1. Some of the labels have been missed off this diagram of Sid's machine. Can you fill them in?

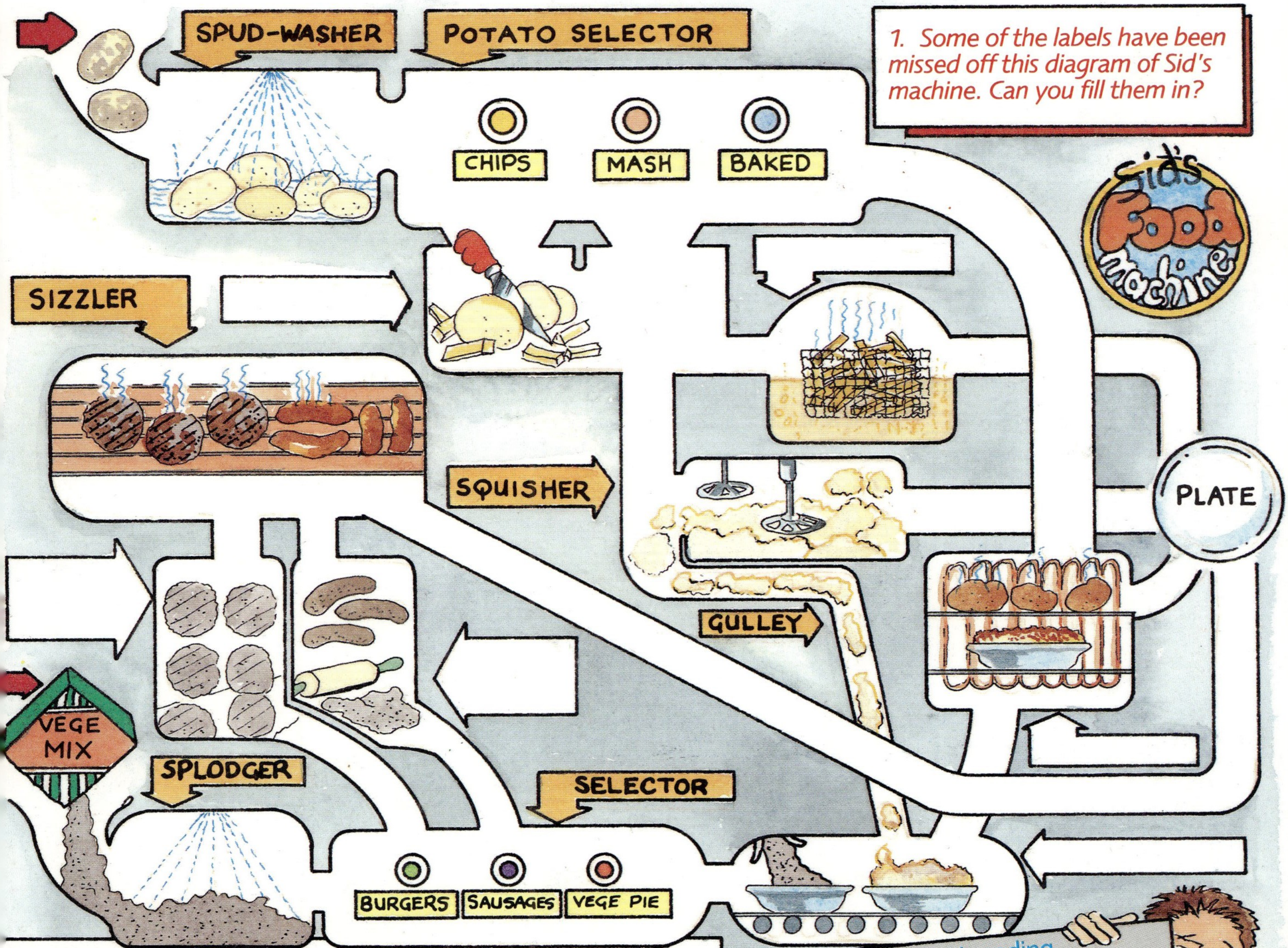

CHIPS   MASH   BAKED

Sid's Food Machine

SIZZLER

SQUISHER

PLATE

GULLEY

VEGE MIX

SPLODGER

SELECTOR

BURGERS   SAUSAGES   VEGE PIE

2. Now you could draw a line through the machine to show how each of these three meals is made. Check you're right on page 22.

Shepherd's Vege Pie   **sausages and mash**   **burgers and baked potato**

Use a different coloured pen for each meal.

How good are you at reading instructions? Make sure you've written in all the **labels** first. When you draw in the routes, make sure you've got **each step right!**

13

Aliens

Read this story. What would you do if something like this happened to you?

One afternoon Mary Ford was driving along an empty country lane. Suddenly her car lost power. It stopped by the side of a field.

There was a flash. The light was so bright it hurt her eyes.

Then she saw it — a huge round machine. It was in the middle of the field. All the grass around it was burnt black.

Two people seemed to float through the side of the machine. They came towards her. They were about 5 metres tall. They wore metal helmets. These came down over their eyes. She could see their eyes through two small slits. They wore a kind of metal overall. It covered all of them, except their hands. Three of their fingers were joined together by a flap of skin.

They opened the car door. She tried to get away. But she could not move. They lifted her up and put her gently on the ground. They did not speak at all. Their faces looked blank.

They moved something over her body. It looked like a large metal eye. They took her left hand. They made three small pin pricks in her thumb. She did not feel anything. They put the blood in a bottle. Mary fainted. When she woke up, she was back in her car. The machine and the aliens had gone.

Later Mary decides to tell the police what had happened that afternoon. She tells them what she can remember.

1. *The story tells us what **really** happened. Here are the things that Mary remembers. Use ticks to say if the things she remembers are **true**, or **false** or if you **can't say**. We've done the first one for you. Check your answers on page 22.*

	What Mary remembers	TRUE	FALSE	CAN'T SAY	REASON
1	They had three toes on each foot.			✓	*Can't say because metal overall covered whole body.*
2	They seemed angry.				
3	I could smell burning.				
4	They couldn't speak English.				
5	They didn't have any eyes.				
6	They were much taller than me.				
7	The machine had a large door.				
8	They didn't hurt me.				

2. Now see if you can give a reason for each answer. We've written one in.

The new waiter

I've just put this advert in the Ghoul End News.

WANTED

Waiter for Gargoyle's Guest House. Must be greasy. Must work long hours. Must not mind if guests are rude. Likely to get bitten.

Gargoyle had two replies.

3, Drain Steet,
Ghoul End
2/11/94

The Manager,
Gargoyle's Guest House,
3, Rodent Avenue,
Ghoul End

Dear Sir,

I would like the job of waiter at your guest house. I have worked at a maggot farm. I have never been a waiter but I am keen to learn.

I am very hard-working and very smelly. I am twenty-one years of age.

Yours faithfully

J. T. Stink

P.S. I like animals – my mum keeps rats.
P.P.S. I don't mind being hit.

The Manager
Gargoyle's Guest House,
3, Rodent Avenue,
Ghoul End

The Ratz Hotel
Ghoul End

3rd November

Dear Sir

I wish to apply for the job of waiter at your guest house. I have worked as a waiter for many years. I used to work for Lord and Lady Ghoul of Ghoul End Hall. I am now head waiter at the Ratz Hotel. Lots of important ghouls come here.

I would like to work in a small family hotel now.

Yours faithfully
Mr. A. P. Slime

Gargoyle asks Mr. Stink and Mr. Slime to come and see him. He asks them both the same questions.

Can you work out who gives which reply? Draw a line from each speech bubble to either Mr. Stink or Mr. Slime.

What would you do if a customer complained that there were not enough flies in his soup?

A. I would get him some more.

B. I would tell him to go somewhere else.

What would you do if an angry customer poured his worm curry over your head?

C. I would send him the bill for having my suit cleaned.

D. I would say 'Thank you very much, sir.'

What would you do if a customer tried to leave without paying his bill?

E. I would lie down in the doorway until you came, sir.

F. I would make him do the washing up.

The two letters tell you things about the characters of Mr. Stink and Mr. Slime — what they're like. Those things will help you work out who said what. I know which Gargoyle will choose. Do you?

You'll find the answers on page 22.

The lost loot

We found this letter in Grandad's house! It's got a bit torn stuffed in this teapot spout but we'll work out where that loot is. I've found a map too which will help.

Dear Gus,
    The police are on to me. Follow these instructions and you'll find the loot.
    Keep some of it for me!
    Take a number 22 .... to Parkside ....
    Then get off at the first stop past the ....
    (I'll probably be inside!) Turn right into.................. Street
    Now turn .... again into .... Lane.
    Walk past the .... and ....(Don't go in for a drink!)
    Take the second .... on the left. You're now in .... Street. The first building on the right is the .... You'll find the .... buried in the .... under the goal posts.

                    Love
                    Grandad

1. Look at the map Gus found. Can you use it to fill in the missing words in Grandad's note? Look at page 22 to check your answers.

18

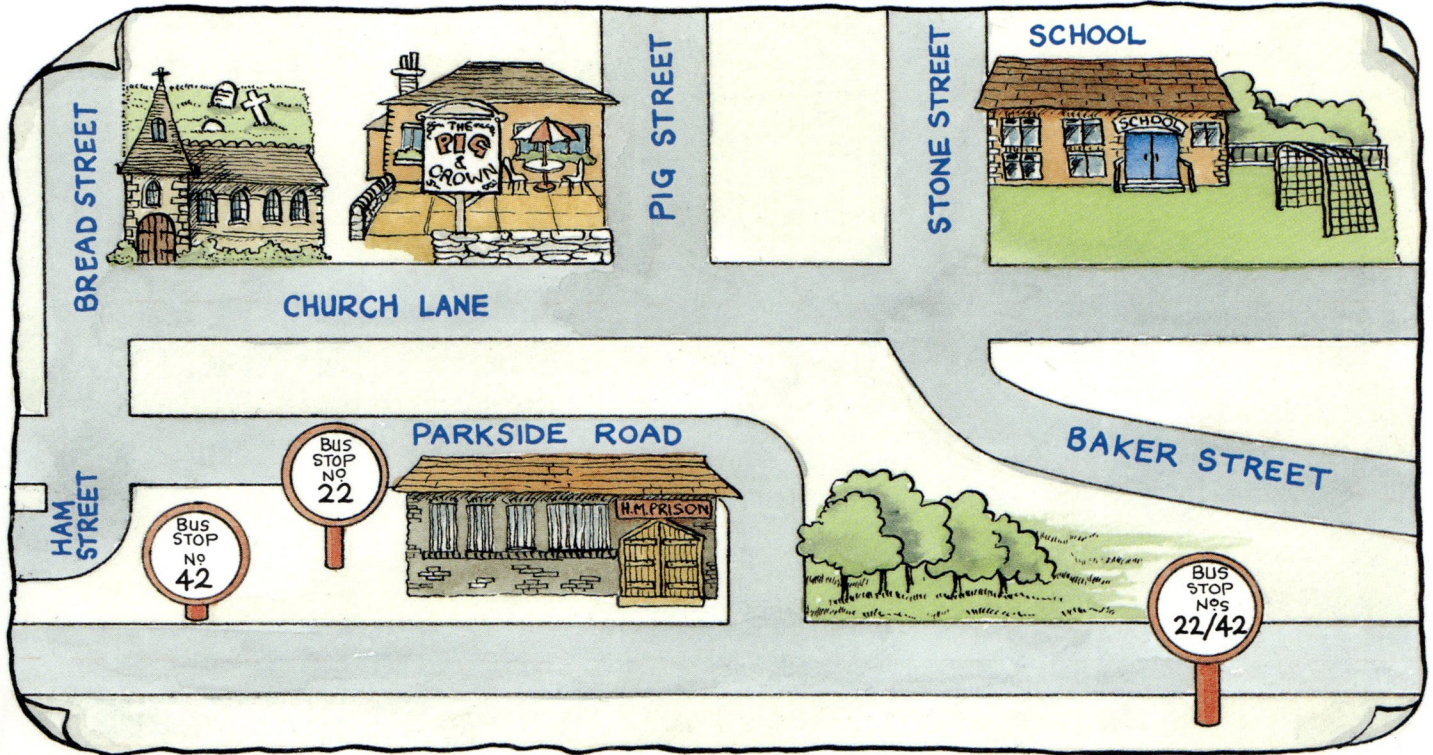

I took the team fishing today. Of course they all complained but everyone caught a fish.

Who caught which fish? Read the four descriptions on the next page carefully, find the clues and fill in the table.

Mr. U's fish is green with some white spots. It swims near the top of the water with its mouth open. It feeds on insects. It is a long thin fish. Mr. U threw it back in the water.

Myrtle's fish is long and thin, but it's blue. It swims near the top of the water, but it keeps its mouth closed. It has no spots.

Cannibal is pleased with his fish. It's a short, fat one with a blue body and white spots. It always swims near the bottom. It keeps its mouth wide open, always looking for food — just like Cannibal!

Feetman's fish is the same shape as Cannibal's. It is the same colour as Mr. U's fish, but it has no spots. It always swims near the bottom, with its mouth closed.

Try to complete this table. It will help you to see who caught which fish. We've done one for you.

	colour	shape	has it got spots?	swims at top or bottom?	mouth open or shut?
Mr. U	green	long & thin	Yes	top	Open
Myrtle					
Cannibal					
Feetman					

Now see if you can draw lines on the picture from the end of each rod to the right fish. Look at page 22 to see if you're right.

Answer page

Crossed wires

Claudia	Weedy
Reshma	Mark
Paul	Keng Tak
Lisa	Tricia
Sid	Ali

Mixed-up rooms

Mrs. Leech — Room 31

Mr. and Mrs. Haunt — Room 34

Mr. W.E.R.E. Wolf — Room 3

Mr. Dungeon — Room 32

Howling Hank

Frame 1 — 3
Frame 2 — 4
Frame 3 — 1
Frame 4 — 6
Frame 5 — 2
Frame 6 — 5

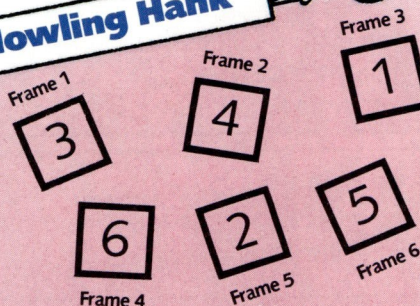

Roxy Rockstar's diamonds

Plan A — Picture 3
Plan B — Picture 1
Plan C — Picture 2
Plan D — Picture 4

Sid's food machine

1. **Shepherd's Vege Pie**

Potatoes — spud-washer, selector, slitter, squisher, gulley, pie-plonker, scorcher
Vege mix — splodger, selector, ⟶ pie-plonker, scorcher

2. **Sausages and mash**

Potatoes — spud-washer, selector, slitter, squisher
Vege mix — splodger, selector, banger-basher, sizzler

3. **Burgers and baked potatoes**

Potatoes — spud-washer, selector, scorcher
Vege mix — splodger, selector, burger-basher, sizzler

Aliens

Numbers 3, 6 and 8 were true. Numbers 2 and 5 were false. We can't say if numbers 1, 4 or 7 were true or false.

The new waiter

Mr. Stink says **A**, **D** and **E**;
Mr. Slime says **B**, **C** and **F**

The lost loot

The missing words are:

bus	Road	prison
Bread	right	Church
'Pig' and 'Crown'		
road	Stone	school
loot	playing field	

The B Team go fishing

Mr. U

Cannibal

Myrtle

Feetman

Check your reading powers! ____

1. On what pages can you find these people?

Fane (page ____)

some bones (page ____)

J.T. Stink (page ____)

a cactus (page ____)

Mary Ford (page ____)

a No. 22 bus (page ____)

2. These are the ten activities in this book.

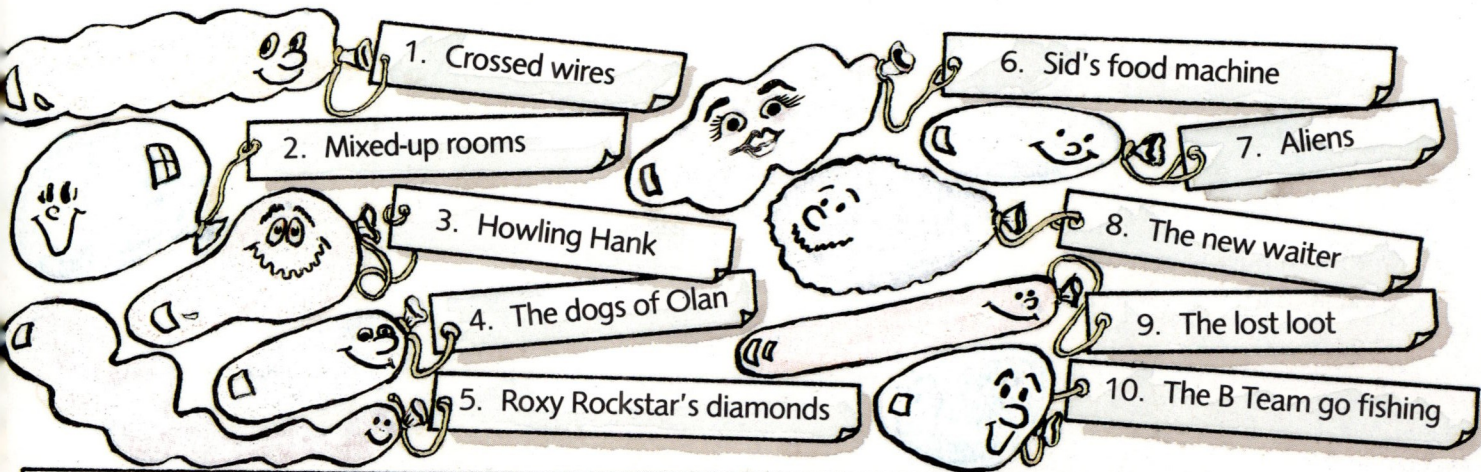

1. Crossed wires

2. Mixed-up rooms

3. Howling Hank

4. The dogs of Olan

5. Roxy Rockstar's diamonds

6. Sid's food machine

7. Aliens

8. The new waiter

9. The lost loot

10. The B Team go fishing

Get your colouring pens, and choose the balloons you want to colour:
use **RED** for the activity you enjoyed most,
use **GREEN** for the activity you thought was the most difficult,
use **BLUE** for the activity you did best.
Then choose your nastiest colour and use it for the activity you thought was the worst.

3. How good do you think you are at understanding what you read?

Tick the answer that seems to be right.

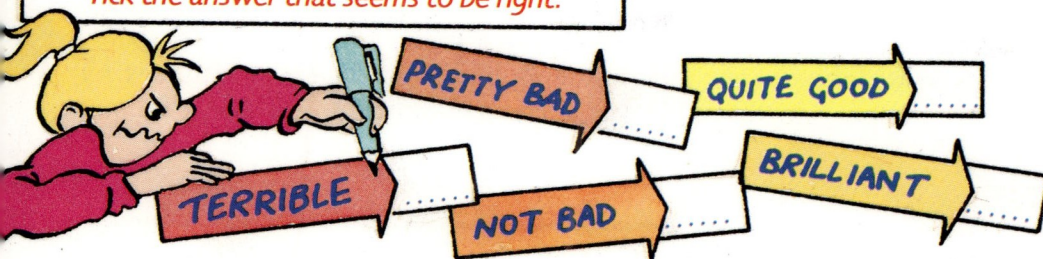

PRETTY BAD

QUITE GOOD

TERRIBLE

NOT BAD

BRILLIANT

Now show this page to your mum or dad. Ask them to read page 24.

23

HOW THIS BOOK *works*

Sit down together to look at the book. Read the advice on page 2 and then begin one activity to get the feel of it. Look at the other pages too — there's lots of **FUN**.

Once started, **PRAISE** your child's first efforts, then just let them work independently. One of the great things about ***SUCCESS!*** is that you don't have to be there all the time. Do make sure, though, that you're around if your child needs your help or wants to show you what they've done.

HOW TO *CHECK* YOUR CHILD'S READING POWERS

When most of the activities are finished suggest that your child tries page 23.

How well did your child do in answering the first set of questions? These are straightforward questions of the kind found in traditional school tests.

How did your child feel about the other activities in the book? Teachers today often prefer to set

PROBLEM-SOLVING QUESTIONS like these. Let your child show you the one they enjoyed most as well as the one they think they did best.

Most of the activities are about right (and are fun too!) for 9-10 year olds. There are more difficult ones too, for example, 'Roxy Rockstar's diamonds' and 'Sid's food machine'. Which one did your child find the most difficult?

HOW *you* CAN HELP

● Encourage your child to ***think*** about what they read. When you find incorrect answers, don't correct them immediately. Make suggestions, get the thinking started — that's what real comprehension is about.

● Encourage your child to ***read lots of books*** — don't worry about the quality all the time. If you want some guidance on good books look at the list in the Essential Parent's Guide.

● How did your child answer question 3 on page 23? Your child's attitude to reading, their ***confidence***, is all important. ***Build up confidence*** by encouraging your child to try the easier activities, for example, 'Howling Hank' and 'The new waiter' — and praise their efforts.

You don't have to be an expert to make a *Success!*